The Children & Young Persons Act 2008

Fergus Smith

B.Sc.(Hons), M.A., C.Q.S.W., D.M.S., Dip.M

Children Act Enterprises Ltd
Pantiles Langham Road
Robertsbridge
East Sussex TN32 5EP
tel: 01580 880243

www.caeuk.org

© Fergus Smith 2008

British Library Cataloguing in Publication Data
A catalogue record for this book is available from the
British Library

ISBN 978-1-899986-03-3

Designed and typeset by Andrew Haig & Associates
Printed in the UK by The Lavenham Press

CAE is an independent organisation which publishes
guides to family and criminal law and provides
consultancy, research, training and independent
investigation services to the public, private and voluntary
sectors.

Contents

All references unless otherwise stated are to the Children & Young Persons Act 2008

Introduction

- This guide is designed for use by social workers, foster carers, teachers, health staff, police and volunteers who work directly or indirectly with children and young persons in the care system.

- The guide provides easy access to and reinforces understanding of the Children & Young Persons Act 2008. This Act gained Royal Assent on 13.11.08, and (except where otherwise indicated) applies to England *and* Wales.

- The background to this Act is that in 2006, the government published proposed improvements to the care system in a Green Paper *'Care Matters: Transforming the Lives of Children and Young People in Care'* and sought responses – see *www.dcsf.gov.uk/consultations*

- In June 2007, a White Paper *'Care Matters: Time for Change'* was published see- *www.dcsf.gov.uk/publications/timeforchange* . This included a commitment to amend primary law, regulations, statutory guidance and national minimum standards.

- The Act is an important part of the government's programme to ensure that children and young people receive high quality care and support.

Key Points

- The Children & Young Persons Act 2008:

  - Enables a local authority to delegate functions for looked after children to providers of social work services and (following a pilot stage) to enable regulation of providers and to require them to be registered under Part 2 of the Care Standards Act 2000 – 'social work surgeries'
  - Places a general duty on the Secretary of State to promote the well-being of children in England
  - Makes provision for the accommodation and maintenance of looked after children and provides powers to make further provision in relation to their placement by regulation including a new power to create a mechanism for the independent review of decisions by fostering service providers that a prospective or existing foster parent is not suitable to foster (similar to current arrangements for prospective adopters)
  - Requires local authorities to take steps to secure sufficient accommodation in their area appropriate for the needs of their looked after children
  - Amends the duties of local authorities in relation to the appointment of independent reviewing officers (IROs); adds to their functions and provides powers for the appropriate national authority to establish a new national IRO service

- independent of local authorities in England and Wales respectively
- Places a new duty on local authorities to appoint a representative to visit all looked after children, wherever they are living and provides a power to extend the duty to other groups of children who were looked after but have ceased to be so
- Extends the duty on local authorities to appoint an independent person to visit, befriend and advise any looked after child if doing so is in her/his interests
- Places a duty on governing bodies of maintained schools to designate a member of staff as having responsibility for promoting the educational achievement of registered pupils who are looked after
- Extends the duty on local authorities to appoint a personal adviser and keep the pathway plan under regular review, to young people who are former relevant children (i.e. care leavers over 18) and who start or resume a programme of education or training after the age of 21 but under the age of 25 years
- Requires local authorities to pay a bursary to a former relevant child who goes on to Higher Education
- Extends the powers of local authorities to make cash payments to children in need and their families
- Adds the provision of short breaks for those who care for disabled children and services to support

family contact for children who are provided with accommodation under health or education legislation to the range of services that local authorities must provide for children and their families;

- Makes provision to enable registration authorities to issue compliance notices to children's home providers failing to meet required standards and to serve a notice preventing new admissions to establishments if this is deemed appropriate;

- Repeals s.45(9) Children Act 989 Act to remove the 72-hour moratorium on the court's powers to hear an application to discharge an Emergency Protection Order

- Places a duty on registrars of births and deaths to notify Local Safeguarding Children Boards (LSCBs) of the particulars of the death of a child and gives the Registrar General power to supply information about the deceased child to the appropriate national authority for research purposes

- Extends the powers of the Secretary of State to carry out research on the functions of local authorities to functions added under recent legislation, in particular the Adoption and Children Act 2002, Children Act 2004 and the Children and Young Persons Act 2008

- Extends the period within which a registration scheme may be established for private fostering by 3 years

- Extends the rights of relatives who are entitled to apply for a Residence or Special Guardianship Order without leave of the court to those with whom the child has lived for a continuous period of 1 year, and ensures that if a court makes a Residence Order, it will normally continue until the child reaches the age of 18

DELIVERY OF SOCIAL WORK SERVICES FOR CHILDREN & YOUNG PERSONS

Power to Enter into Arrangements for Discharge of Care Functions [s.1]

■ A local authority may (subject to s.2 described below) enter into arrangements with a 'corporate body' for the discharge by that body of some or all of its:

   • Social services functions in relation to individual children who are 'looked after' by it and
   • Functions under s.23B to 24D of the 1989 Act (i.e. former relevant children) [s.1(1);(2)]

■ A party (*other* than the local authority concerned) to arrangements entered into under s.1:

   • May not include any other local authority and
   • Is referred to in Part 1 as a 'provider of social work services' [s.1(3)]

   NB. Regulations may be made about corporate bodies that may or may not be parties to arrangements under s.1 [s.1 (7)].

■ Arrangements under s.1 may be framed by reference to:

   • Individuals of a particular description
   • Particular localities within the area of the local authority concerned [s.1(4)]

■ When an individual child (A) ceases to be looked after by a local authority and a provider of social work services (P) was discharging, under arrangements under Part 1, social services functions of the authority in relation to A at that time, the arrangements may also make provision for P to discharge all or any of the authority's social services functions in relation to her/him after s/he ceases to be looked after by the authority [s.1(5)]

■ The 'appropriate national authority' (in England the Secretary of State and in Wales, the Welsh Ministers) *may* by regulations specify functions:

- Not falling within s.1(2) which are though, to be treated as being 'relevant care functions' for the purposes of s.1
- Otherwise falling within s.1(2) which are to be treated as *not* being relevant care functions for the purposes of s.1 [s.1(6);(11)]

NB. The appropriate national authority may also by regulations make provision about the 'bodies corporate' which may, or may not, be parties to arrangements under s.1[s.1(7)] and regulate so that arrangements under s.1 may not be entered into for a period shorter than the prescribed minimum or for a period exceeding the prescribed maximum [s.1(8)].

Restrictions on Arrangements under s.1 [s.2]

■ A local authority must not enter into arrangements under s.1 for the discharge of an 'excluded function', i.e.:

- The local authority's functions in relation to independent reviewing officers (IROs) and
- Its functions as an adoption agency (unless the other party to the arrangements is a registered adoption society) [s.2(1);(2)]

NB. The functions with respect to IROs are the local authority's functions under regulations made under s.26 Children Act1989 Act by virtue of s.26(2)(k) (provision for appointment by local authority of a person to carry out certain functions in review of case of child looked after by the authority), s 25A of the 1989 Act (appointment of independent reviewing officer) [s.2(3)].

Any restriction imposed on a local authority by reference to its area applies to a provider of social work services as if it has the same area as the authority [s.2(4)].

■ A local authority must not enter into arrangements under section 1 unless it is satisfied that the functions to which the arrangements relate will be discharged by, or under the supervision of, registered social workers [s.2(5)].

Effect of Arrangements under s.1 [s.3]

■ Anything done or not done by, or in relation to a provider of social work services under s.1 will be treated as done or not done by the local authority which entered into the arrangements [s.3(1)].

■ The provision introduced by s.3(1):

- Does not affect the rights and liabilities of the parties to arrangements as between one another
- Does not make the local authority liable under s.6 Human Rights Act 1998 in respect of any act (within the meaning of that section) of a provider of social work services of a 'private nature'
- Does not prevent any civil proceedings which could otherwise be brought by or against the provider of the services from being brought and
- Does not apply for the purposes of any criminal proceedings brought in respect of anything done or omitted to be done by the provider of social work services [s.3(2)]

■ A reference in s.3 to anything done or not done by, or in relation to a provider of social work services includes a reference to an act or omission of an employee or agent of the provider [s.3(3)].

NB. Thus, the provider and the local authority may be equally liable for the acts of a provider.

S.4 (regulation of providers of social work services and s.5
    (functions under Part 1 to be 'social services
    functions') are of insufficient operational relevance
    and have not been included.

Piloting & Expiry of Arrangements Under Part 1 [s.6]

■ The piloting period for the arrangements allowed under Part 1 of this Act:

- Begins on the day on which s.1(1) comes into force and
- Ends when s.4 comes into force; *or* if it is earlier, 5 years after this Act is passed [s.6(1)]

■ An order bringing s.1 into force may do so by reference to particular local authorities or local authorities of a particular description [s.6 (2)].

NB. Sections 1–5 cease to have effect if the piloting period is terminated automatically after 5 years i.e. before s.4 (introducing regulation of social work providers) is brought into force and [s.6(3)-(5)]. Regulations under s.1(8) may not be made to come into force before the pilot period ends and arrangements entered into in the pilot period must not last for more than 5 years after this Act is passed [s.6(6)].

PART 2

FUNCTIONS IN RELATION TO CHILDREN & YOUNG PERSONS

Well-being

Well-being of Children and Young Persons [s.7]

■ It is the general duty of the Secretary of State to promote the well-being of children in England [s.7(1)].

■ The general duty imposed by s.7(1) is subject to any specific duties imposed on the Secretary of State [s.7(2)].

■ The activities which may be undertaken or supported in the discharge of the general duty imposed by s.7(1) include activities in connection with parenting [s.7(3)].

NB. This would include parental care provided by any person, not just that provided by a parent / other person who has parental responsibility.

■ The Secretary of State may take such action as s/he considers appropriate to promote the well-being of persons receiving services under s.23C to 24D Children Act 1989 (i.e. specified care leavers) and those aged less than 25 years old of a prescribed description [s.7(4)].

NB. The Secretary of State under s.7 must have regard to the aspects of well-being mentioned in s.10 (2) (a) to (e) Children Act 2004 [s.7 (5)] i.e. physical and mental health and emotional well-being, protection from harm and neglect, education, training and recreation, their contribution to society and

*economic well-being. S.7 came into force on 13.11.08
when the Act received Royal Assent.*

Accommodation

Provision of Accommodation, & Maintenance for Children Looked After by a Local Authority [s.8]

■ By virtue of s.8(1), s.23 Children Act 1989 is substituted as follows by:

- **Provision of accommodation for children in care:** when a child is in the care of a local authority, it is its duty to provide her/him with accommodation [s.22A Children Act 1989]
- **Maintenance of looked after children**: it is the duty of a local authority to maintain a child it is looking after in other respects apart from the provision of accommodation [s.22B Children Act 1989]

■ S.22C (**ways in which looked after children are to be accommodated and maintained**) applies as follows when a local authority is looking after a child C [s.22C (1) Children Act 1989].

■ The local authority must make arrangements for C to live with a person who falls within s.22C (3) (but subject to s.22C(4)) [s.22C(2) Children Act 1989].

■ A person (P) falls within subsection 22C(3) if:

- P is a parent of C
- P is *not* a parent of C but has parental responsibility for her/him; or

- In a case when C is in the care of the local
  authority and there was a Residence Order in
  force with respect her/him immediately before
  the care order was made, P was a person in
  whose favour that order was made [s.22C(3)
  Children Act 1989]

  *NB. S.22C(2) does not require the local authority to
  make arrangements of the kind mentioned in that
  subsection if doing so would not be consistent with
  C's welfare or would not be reasonably practicable
  [s.22C(4) Children Act 1989].*

- ■ If the local authority is unable to make arrangements
  under s.22C (2), it must place C in the placement
  which is, in its opinion, the most appropriate
  placement available [s.22C(5) Children Act 1989].

- ■ In s.22C(5) 'placement' means placement:

  - With an individual who is a relative, friend or
    other person connected with C and who is also a
    local authority foster parent
  - With a local authority foster parent who does not
    fall within the above category
  - In a children's home in respect of which a person
    is registered under Part 2 Care Standards Act
    2000; or
  - (Subject to section 22D), placement in
    accordance with other arrangements which
    comply with any regulations made for the
    purposes of s.22 [s.22C(6) Children Act 1989]

- In determining the most appropriate placement for C, the local authority must, subject to other provisions of this Part (in particular, duties under s.22 Children Act 1989):

  - Give preference to a placement falling within the first paragraph in s.22C(6) above over placements falling within the other 3 paragraphs of that section
  - Comply, so far as is reasonably practicable in all the circumstances of C's case, with the requirements of s.22C(8) and
  - Comply with s.22C(9) unless that is not reasonably practicable [s.22C(7) Children Act 1989]

- The local authority must ensure the placement is such that:

  - It allows C to live near C's home
  - It does not disrupt C's education or training
  - If C has a sibling for whom the local authority is also providing accommodation, it enables C and the sibling to live together
  - If C is disabled, the accommodation provided is suitable to C's particular needs [s.22C(8) Children Act 1989]

- The placement must be such that C is provided with accommodation within the local authority's area [s.22C (9) Children Act 1989].

- The local authority may determine the terms:

  - Of any arrangements its makes under s.22C(2) in relation to C (including terms as to payment); and
  - On which it places C with a local authority foster parent (including terms as to payment but subject to any order made under s.49 Children Act 2004) [s.22C(10) Children Act 1989]

  NB. The appropriate national authority may make regulations for, and in connection with, the purposes of s.22 [s.22C (11) Children Act 1989].

- **22D (review of child's case before making alternative arrangements for accommodation) provides that:**

  - When a local authority is providing accommodation for a child (C) other than by arrangements under s.22C(6)(d), it must not make such arrangements for her/him unless it has decided to do so in consequence of a review of C's case carried out in accordance with regulations made under s.26 Children Act 1989

  NB. S.22D(1) does not prevent a local authority making arrangements for C under s.22C(6)(d) if it is satisfied that in order to safeguard her/his welfare it is necessary to make such arrangements and to do so as a matter of urgency [s.22D(2).

- **22E (children's homes provided by appropriate national authority) provides that:**

  - When a local authority place a child it is looking after in a children's home provided, equipped and maintained by an appropriate national authority under s.82(5), it must do so on such terms as that national authority may from time to time determine

- **22F (regulations as to children looked after by local authorities) provides that** Part 2 of Schedule 2 has effect for the purposes of making further provision as to children looked after by local authorities and in particular as to the regulations which may be made under s.22C(11).

- Schedule 1 (which makes amendments supplementary to, and consequential on, the provisions of s.22 including a power to make regulations about an 'independent review mechanism' for certain decisions in relation to foster parents) has effect [s.8 (2)].

  NB. Until s.8(1) comes into force, Sch.2 to the Children Act 1989 has effect with those modifications specified in Sch.2 of this Act [s.8(3)].

General Duty of Local Authority to Secure Sufficient Accommodation [s.9]

■ S.9 inserts after s.22F Children Act 1989 (inserted by s.8), a s.22G (**general duty of local authority to secure sufficient accommodation for looked after children**) as follows:

- It is the general duty of a local authority to take steps that secure, so far as reasonably practicable, the outcome in s.22G(2) [s.22G(1) Children Act 1989]
- The outcome is that the local authority is able to provide the children mentioned in s.22G(3) with accommodation that is within the authority's area; and meets the needs of those children [s.22G(2) Children Act 1989]

■ The children referred to in s.22G(2) are those:

- The local authority is looking after
- In respect of whom the authority is unable to make arrangements under s.22C(2), and
- Whose circumstances are such that it would be consistent with their welfare for them to be provided with accommodation that is in the authority's area [s.22G(3) Children Act 1989]

■ In taking steps to secure the outcome in s.22G(2), the local authority must have regard to the benefit of having:

- A number of accommodation providers in its area that is, in its opinion, sufficient to secure that outcome and
- A range of accommodation in its area capable of meeting different needs that is, in its opinion, sufficient to secure that outcome [s.22G(4) Children Act 1989]

Independent Reviewing Officers

Appointment of Independent Reviewing Officer [s.25A Children Act 1989 introduced by s.10(1)]

■ s.10(1) inserts, after s.25 Children Act 1989 a s.25A (**appointment of independent reviewing officer**) and means that:

- If a local authority is looking after a child, it must appoint an individual as the independent reviewing officer (IRO) for that child's case
- The initial appointment under s.25A(1) must be made before the child's case is first reviewed in accordance with regulations made under s.26
- If a vacancy arises in respect of a child's case, the local authority must make another appointment under s.25A (1) as soon as is practicable.
- An appointee must be of a description prescribed in regulations made by the appropriate national authority [s.25A]

Functions of the IRO [s.25B Children Act 1989 introduced by s.10 (1)]

■ s.10(1) further inserts a s.25B (**functions of the independent reviewing officer**) and means that:

- The IRO must monitor the performance by the local authority of its functions in relation to the child's case, participate, in accordance with regulations made by the appropriate national authority in any review of the child's **case**, ensure that any ascertained wishes and feelings of the child concerning the case are given due consideration by the local authority, and perform any other function which is prescribed in regulations made by the appropriate national authority [s.25B(1)]

NB. The duty to monitor local authority performance with respect to the 'case' is wider than the current IRO role which is limited to the review functions.

- An IRO's functions must be performed in such manner (if any) as may be prescribed in regulations made by the appropriate national authority and having regard to such guidance as that authority may issue in relation to the discharge of those functions [s.25B(2)]
- If the IRO considers it appropriate to do so, the child's case may be referred by that officer to an officer of the Children and Family Court Advisory

and Support Service (CAFCASS) or a Welsh family proceedings officer [s.25B(3)]

■ If the IRO is not an officer of the local authority, it is the duty of the authority to co-operate with that individual and to take all such reasonable steps as that individual may require of them to enable that individual's functions under s.25B to be performed satisfactorily [s.25B(4)]

Referred Cases [s.25C Children Act 1989 introduced by s.10(1)]

- s.10(1) also inserts a s.25C (**referred cases**) and:
  - Means that in relation to children whose cases are referred to officers under s.25B(3), the Lord Chancellor may by regulations extend any functions of the officers in respect of family proceedings (within the meaning of s.12 of the Criminal Justice and Court Services Act 2000 to other proceedings
  - Requires any functions of the officers to be performed in the manner prescribed by the regulations (yet to be made)

NB. The power to make regulations in s.25C Children Act is exercisable in relation to functions of Welsh family proceedings officers only with the consent of the Welsh Ministers [s.25C(2) introduced by s.10(1)]

Power to Make Further Provision Concerning Independent Reviewing Officers: England [s.11]

■ The Secretary of State may by order:

- Establish a corporate body to discharge such functions as may be conferred on it by order or
- Confer functions on CAFCASS [s.11(1)]

■ An order under s.11 may confer functions in relation to England in connection with any or all of the following matters (but no others):

- Provision of training for persons appointed or to be appointed as independent reviewing officers
- Accreditation of persons as independent reviewing officers
- Appointment of persons as independent reviewing officers
- Management of persons appointed or accredited as independent reviewing officers [s.11(2)]

■ An order under s.11 which establishes a corporate body may provide that the:

- Body is to be subject to inspection by the chief inspector and may for that purpose apply (with or without modification) any provision of the Education and Inspections Act 2006 [s.11(3)]

- Functions of the body must be performed in accordance with directions given by the Secretary of State [s.12(4)]

NB. In s.11, 'accreditation' means the process by which a person qualifies for and remains qualified for appointment as an independent reviewing officer; 'chief inspector' means Her Majesty's Chief Inspector of Education, Children's Services and Skills' and the 'Service' means CAFCASS [s.11(5)]

This power will be used to establish a national IRO service if amendments introduced by s.10 do not prove to be effective in achieving significant improvements in outcomes for looked after children.

Power to Make Further Provision Concerning Independent Reviewing Officers: Wales [s.12]

■ The Welsh Ministers may by order:

- Establish a corporate body to discharge such functions as may be conferred on it by the order or
- Provide for the discharge by them of such functions as may be conferred on them by the order [s.12(1)]

■ An order under s.12 may confer functions in relation to Wales in connection with any or all of the following matters (but no others):

- Provision of training for persons appointed or to be appointed as IROs
- Accreditation of persons as IROs
- Appointment of persons as IROs
- Management of persons appointed or accredited as IROs [s.12(2)]

■ An order under s.12 in consequence of the conferral of a function by the order, modify any provision made by or under an enactment:

- Relating to independent reviewing officers
- Where the function is conferred on the Welsh Ministers, relating to those Ministers [s.12(3)]

■ An order under s.12 which establishes a corporate body may provide that:

- The body is to be subject to inspection by an independent inspector specified in or established by the order, and may for that purpose apply (with or without modifications) any enactment relating to the carrying out of inspections
- The functions of the body must be performed in accordance with directions given by the Welsh Ministers [s.12(4)]

NB. In s.12 'accreditation' has the same meaning as in s.11 [s.12 (5)].

Orders under ss.11 & 12: Supplementary Provisions [s.13]

- The conferral of any function by an order under ss.11 or 12(1)(a) also confers on the recipient power to do anything which is incidental or conducive to, or designed to facilitate, the discharge of that function [s.13(1)]

- An order under ss.11 or 12 may authorise the recipient to charge fees for the discharge by it of any function conferred by the order [s.13 (2)].

- An order under ss.11 or 12 may transfer property, rights and liabilities to the recipient (and may also provide that anything which might otherwise prevent, penalise or restrict such a transfer is not to do so) [s.13(3)].

- When an order makes provision by virtue of s.13(3) in relation to rights and liabilities relating to an employee it must make provision for the Transfer of Undertakings (Protection of Employment) Regulations 2006 to apply to that transfer [s.13(4)].

- An order under ss.11 or 12 may require the recipient to establish a procedure for dealing with complaints relating to the discharge by it of its functions [s.13 (5)].

  NB. In s.13 'recipient' means, in relation to a function, the body on which the function is conferred by the order in question, and for this purpose 'body' includes the Welsh Ministers [s.13(6)].

Expiry of Powers Conferred by ss.11 & 12 [s.14]

■ If no order has been made under s.11 by the relevant time, that section and s.13 so far as it applies for the purposes of that section, cease to have effect [s.14(1)].

■ If no order has been made under s.12 by the relevant time, that section, and s.13 so far as it applies for the purposes of that section, cease to have effect [s.14(2)].

NB. The 'relevant time' is the end of the period of 7 years beginning with the day on which this Act is passed –i.e. 13.11.08 [s.14 (3)].

Visiting

Duty of Local Authority to Ensure Visits to Looked After Children & Others [s.15]

- S.15 introduces a s.23ZA to the Children Act 1989 which applies to a:

  - Child looked after by a local authority
  - A child or young person who was looked after but who has ceased to be looked after by it as a result of prescribed circumstances [s.23ZA(1)]

- It is the duty of the local authority to:

  - Ensure that a person to whom s.23 applies is visited by a 'representative' of the authority
  - Arrange for appropriate advice, support and assistance to be available to a person to whom s.23 applies who seeks it from that local authority [s.23ZA(2) inserted by s.13]

- The duties imposed by s.23ZA(2) are to be discharged in accordance with any regulations made for the purposes of this section by the appropriate national authority and are subject to any requirement imposed by or under an enactment applicable to the place in which the person to whom this section applies is accommodated (e.g. in custody or detained under the Mental Health Act) [s.23ZA(3)].

- Regulations under s.23 for the purposes of the above regulations may make provision about the:

- Frequency of visits
- Circumstances in which a person to whom this section applies must be visited by a representative and
- Functions of a representative [s.23ZA(4)]

■ In choosing a representative a local authority must satisfy themselves that the person chosen has the necessary skills and experience to perform the functions of a representative [s.23ZA(5)].

NB. 'Appropriate national authority' means in England the Secretary of State and in Wales the Welsh Ministers [s.23ZA(6)].

Independent Visitors for Children Looked After by a Local Authority [s.16]

- S.16 inserts a new s.23ZB into the 1989 Act and requires that a local authority looking after a child to appoint an independent person to be the child's visitor if:

  - The child falls within a description prescribed in regulations made by the appropriate national authority or
  - In any other case, it appears to the local authority that it would be in the child's interests to do so [s.23ZB(1)]

  NB. Thus, the group for whom independent visitors must be appointed is extended and current provisions in para. 2 of Sch.17 Children Act 1989 are abolished.

- A person appointed under s.23 must visit, befriend and advise the child [s.23ZB (2)].

- A person appointed under s.23 is entitled to recover from the appointing authority any reasonable expenses incurred by that person for the purposes of that person's functions under s.23 [s.23ZB(3)].

- A person's appointment as a visitor in pursuance of this s.23 comes to an end if the:

  - Child ceases to be looked after by the local authority

- Person resigns the appointment by giving notice in writing to the appointing authority or
- Authority gives notice in writing that it has terminated it [s.23ZB(4)]

■ The ending of such an appointment does not affect any duty under this s.23 to make a further appointment [s.23ZB (5)].

■ If a local authority propose to appoint a visitor for a child under s.23, the appointment shall not be made if the:

- Child objects to it and
- Authority is satisfied s/he has sufficient understanding to make an informed decision [s.23ZB(6)]

■ If a visitor has been appointed for a child under s.23 the local authority must terminate the appointment if the:

- Child objects to its continuing; and
- Authority is satisfied that the child has sufficient understanding to make an informed decision [s.23ZB(7)]

■ If the local authority give effect to a child's objection under s.23ZB(6) or (7) and the objection is to having anyone as the child's visitor, the authority does not have to propose to appoint another person under s.23ZB(1) until the objection is withdrawn [s.23ZB(8)].

NB. The appropriate national authority (in England the Secretary of State; in Wales the Welsh Ministers) may make regulations as to circumstances in which a person is to be regarded for the purposes of s.23 as 'independent' of the appointing authority [s.23ZB (9);(10)].

Notification to Appropriate Officer of Children in Long-Term Care [s.17]

■ S.85 of the 1989 Act (children accommodated by health bodies or local education authorities) is amended so that notifications must be to the 'appropriate officer' (local Director of Children's Services in England and the Lead Director for Children & Young Persons for a local authority in Wales.

Visits to Children in Long-Term Care [s.18]

■ S.18 inserts a new s.86A to the Children Act 1989 (visitors for children notified to local authority under ss.85 or 86) and applies if the appropriate officer of a local authority:

- Has been notified with respect to a child under s. 85(1) (accommodated by health bodies or local education authorities) or 86(1) (care home or independent hospital) and
- Has not been notified with respect to that child under s.85(2) or, as the case may be, 86(2) i.e. that the child has ceased to be so accommodated [s.86A Children Act 1989 as inserted by s.18]

■ The local authority must, in accordance with regulations made under s.86A, make arrangements for the child to be visited by a 'representative' of the authority [s.86A (2)].

■ It is the function of a representative to provide advice and assistance to the local authority on the performance of its duties under s.85(4) or s.86(3) (i.e. to take such steps as are reasonably practicable to enable it to determine whether the child's welfare is adequately safeguarded and promoted and consider the extent to which (if at all) it should exercise any of its functions under the Children Act 1989) [s.86A(3)].

NB. The local authority might conclude that the child is 'in need' as per s.17 Children Act 1989 and requires family support services.

■ Regulations under s.86 Children Act 1989 may make provision about:

- The frequency of visits under visiting arrangements
- Circumstances in which visiting arrangements must require a child to be visited; and
- Additional functions of a representative [s.86A(4) inserted by s.16]

■ Regulations under s.86 are to be made by the Secretary of State and the Welsh Ministers acting jointly [s.86A (5)].

■ In choosing a representative a local authority must satisfy themselves that the person chosen has the necessary skills and experience to perform the functions of a representative [s.86A(6)].

Education & Training

Designated Member of Staff at School for Pupils Looked After by a Local Authority [s.20]

- The governing body of a maintained school must designate a member of the staff at the school (the 'designated person') as having responsibility for promoting the educational achievement of registered pupils at the school who:

  - Are being looked after by a local authority; or
  - Fall within s.20(6) [s.20(1)]

- The governing body must ensure that the designated person undertakes appropriate training [s.20(2)]

- The appropriate national authority may by regulations make provision requiring the governing body of a maintained school to ensure that the designated person has qualifications or experience (or both) prescribed by the regulations [s.20(3)].

  NB. The intention is to use this power to require governing bodies to appoint a qualified teacher to perform this role.

- In exercising its functions under s.20, a governing body of a maintained school must have regard to any guidance issued by the appropriate national authority [s.20(4)].

  NB. It is understood government will update the guidance circulated in England in 2000 – 'The

Education of Children and Young People in Public Care' (and its Welsh equivalent of 2001) and will use this power to issue statutory guidance.

■ For the purposes of s.20(1) a person is 'looked after by a local authority' if s/he is:

- Looked after by a local authority for the purposes of the 1989 Act or the Children (Scotland) Act 1995 or
- Looked after by an authority for the purposes of the Children (Northern Ireland) Order 1995 [s.20(5)].

■ A person falls within s.20(6) if the person:

- Is a 'relevant child' within the meaning of s.23A of the 1989 Act or article 34B of the Children (Northern Ireland) Order 1995
- Is a 'former relevant' child within the meaning of s.23C of the 1989 Act or article 34D of the Children (Northern Ireland) Order 1995 or
- Has been looked after by a local authority for the purposes of the Children (Scotland) Act 1995 at any time after attaining the age of 16 [s.20(6)]

Entitlement to Payment in Respect of Higher Education [s.21]

- S.23C Children Act 1989 (continuing functions of local authorities in respect of 'former relevant children') is amended in accordance with s.21(2) –(4) [s.21(1)].

- The result of these amendments is that in addition to providing assistance under s.23C(4), the local authority will have to pay a fixed sum to those who pursue a higher education course.

- The amount will be determined in regulations, which will also prescribe eligibility criteria, arrangements for making payments (e.g. instalments, intervals between instalments) and circumstances in which instalments may cease or payments be repaid.

- The duty of the local authority to make payments lasts for as long as the young person follows her/his pathway plan (made under s.23B or s.23CA).

  NB. This payment does not affect entitlement to other assistance given under s.23C(4) and will be exempt from tax.

Assistance to Pursue Education or Training [s.22]

■ S.22(1) amends s.23B Children Act 1989 by omitting subsections 4–7 and inserting after s.23C a new s.23CA thus extending the duty of the local authority so that:

- It must appoint a personal adviser for a 'former relevant child' who informs the responsible local authority (i.e. the one that formerly looked after her/him) that s/he is or intends to pursue a programme of education or training but to whom the local authority would not otherwise have a duty under s.23C because s/he is aged over 21 and has completed or abandoned the programme set out in her/his original pathway plan

- In relation to such an individual aged under 25 (or less if the appropriate national authority prescribe this), the local authority must also carry out an assessment of needs, prepare a pathway plan and provide such assistance as the person's educational and training needs require

NB. The local authority may take into account any payment made under s.23C (5A) when making its assessment of needs.

Extension of Entitlements to Personal Adviser and to Assistance in Connection with Education or Training [s.23]

■ S.23 amends s.23D(1) Children Act 1989 so that the power to make regulations (not so far exercised) requiring local authorities to appoint personal advisers for certain groups of young people is amended to:

- Extend the upper end of the age range from 21 to 25 years of age
- Extend the upper end of the age range to which the powers for local authorities to provide assistance toward expenses incurred by a young person in education or training apply to age 25

Cash Payments

Extension of Power to Make Payments in Cash [s.24]

■ S.24 amends s.17(6) Children Act 1989 (nature of services which may be provided by a local authority for children in need, their families and others) so as to omit 'in exceptional circumstances' [s.24(1)].

NB. The declared intention provided by the 'Explanatory Notes' that accompanied publication of this Act is to allow local authorities to exercise a much wider discretion over the circumstances in which they can make cash payments to those caring for children in need e.g. to make regular and continuing payments.

Care Breaks

Breaks from Caring for Disabled Children [s.25]

■ Para.6 of Schedule 2 Children Act 1989 (**provision by local authorities for disabled children**) is amended so that every local authority shall provide services designed to:

- Minimise the effect on disabled children within its area of their disabilities
- Give such children the opportunity to lead lives which are as normal as possible
- Assist individuals who provide care for such children to continue to do so, or to do so more effectively, by giving them breaks from caring

■ The duty imposed by the latter para. shall be performed in accordance with regulations made by the appropriate national authority [Sch.2 para.6 Children Act 1989].

Enforcement of Care Standards

Powers of Chief Inspector, Notice Restricting Accommodation, Appeals & Notifications [ss.26–29]

■ Ss.26–29 amend the Care Standards Act 2000 (itself being amended by Parliament during 2008) and confers additional powers and duties on the registration authority in relation to standards in children's social care settings such as children's homes, fostering agencies, residential family centres, adoption support agencies and voluntary adoption agencies.

■ *In England only*, s.26 introduces a new s.22A into the Care Standards Act 2000 so that the Chief Inspector may serve (on owner / proprietor or registered manager) a 'compliance notice' if of the opinion that an establishment or agency is not meeting the required standard as set out regulations or National Minimum Standards (these standards are currently being reviewed and new ones are due in 2009).

■ A person who in response to such a notice fails to take the required steps will be guilty of a criminal offence and may be fined.

■ S.27 (**notice restricting accommodation at certain establishments**) inserts a new s.22B into the Care Standards Act 2000 so that the Chief Inspector (or in Wales the Welsh Ministers) are enabled to impose a requirement preventing any new admission of children to children's homes and family residential centres (such notices must be served on each person who is registered in respect to the establishment concerned).

■ Such a notice (which may be limited in time and can be revoked) must set out reasons for it and explain the right of appeal.

■ S.28 (appeals etc in relation to notices under s22B Care Standards Act 2000) amends s.21 Care Standards Act 2000 and creates new grounds for appeal to the Tribunal relevant to ss.27.

■ S.29 (**notification of matters relating to persons carrying on children's homes etc**) imposes a duty on the Chief Inspector (in Wales the Welsh Ministers) to notify each local authority in England and Wales if certain enforcement action is taken (this should prompt a local authority that has a residential placement in such an establishment, to review it).

Emergency Protection Orders

Removal of Restriction on Hearing of Application for Discharge of Emergency Protection Order [s.30]

■ S.30 amends s.45 Children Act 1989 Act (emergency protection orders: supplementary provisions) by omitting subsection 9 i.e. it revokes the 72 hour restriction on applying for discharge of an Emergency Protection Order.

NB. This change has been introduced to ensure compatibility with Article 6(1) and 8 of the European Convention on Human Rights (for more detail, see CAE's companion guide Children Act 1989 in the Context of the Human Rights Act 1998)

Information & Research

Supply of Information Concerning the Death of Children to Local Safeguarding Children Boards [s.31]

- If, under the Births and Deaths Registration Act 1953, a registrar of births and deaths registers the death of a person and the registrar believes that the deceased was or may have been under the age of 18 at the time of death, s/he must within 7 days, secure that the appropriate Local Safeguarding Children Board (LSCB) is notified of the particulars of the death entered in the register [s.31 (1);(2);(7)].

- If, under the 1953 Act, an entry in a register kept for a sub-district concerning a death is corrected and the person making the correction believes that the entry relates to a person who was or may have been under the age of 18 at the time of death, s/he must, within 7 days, secure that the appropriate LSCB is notified of the particulars of the death as corrected [s.31(3);(4);(7)].

- If, under the 1953 Act, a registrar of births and deaths issues a certificate to the effect that a death is *not* required by law to be registered in England or Wales but the registrar believes that the deceased was or may have been under the age of 18 at the time of death, s/he must, within 7 days, secure that the LSCB established by the Children's Services Authority within whose area the registrar's sub-district is situated is notified of the:

- Issuing of the certificate; and
- Registrar's belief and the grounds for it [s.31(5);(6);(7)]

NB. The requirements of s.27 do not apply if the death occurred before 01.04.08 [s.31 (8)].

■ Each LSCB must:

- Make arrangements for the receipt by it of notifications under s.31 and
- Publish those arrangements [s.31(9)]

Power of Registrar General to Supply Information to National Authorities [s.32]

- The Registrar General may supply information to which s.32 applies to the Secretary of State, or to the Welsh Ministers, for research purposes [s.32(1)].

- Information supplied under s.32 (1) to the Secretary of State or the Welsh Ministers may be disclosed by them to any other person if disclosure is for research purposes and to a LSCB for the purposes of its functions [s.32(2)]

- S.32 applies to any information that is kept by the Registrar General under any provision made by or under an enactment and relates to the death of a person who was or may have been under the age of 18 at the time of death [s.32(3)].

  NB. For 'research purposes' means for the purposes of any research that is being or may be conducted or assisted under s.83(1) Children Act 1989 [s.32(4)].

Research etc into Matters Connected with Certain Statutory Functions [s.33]

■ S.83 Children Act 1989 Act (research and returns of information) is amended to reflect the existence of Adoption and Children Act 2002, Children Act 2004 and Children and Young Persons Act 2008.

PART 3

ADOPTION & FOSTERING

Independent Review of Determinations Relating to Adoption [s.34]

- S.12 of the Adoption and Children Act 2002 (independent review of determinations) is amended to clarify that the regulations will provide for the application for a review to be made to the appropriate Minister and that the review will be via a panel constituted by that Minster.

- Regulations may be introduced to impose a duty to make a payment to the appropriate Minister to cover the costs (and only the costs) in performing the independent review functions.

Extension of Period allowed for Making Regulations under s.45 or 46 Children Act 1989 [s.35]

- S.47(3) Children Act 2004 (relevant time for expiry of powers under ss. 45;46) is amended so the power under s.45 for the Secretary of State (England) and s.46 (Welsh Ministers) to establish via regulations a scheme for registration of private foster carers is extended so that each government now has until November 2011 to decide if regulations are necessary in its own country.

PART 4

ORDERS UNDER PART 2
CHILDREN ACT 1989

Residence Orders

Entitlement of Relative to Apply for a Residence Order [s.36]

■ S.10 Children Act 1989 (power of the court to make orders under s.8 of that Act), is amended by the insertion of a s.10(5B) as follows:

- 'A relative of a child is entitled (i.e. does not need to seek a court's agreement) to apply for a Residence Order with respect to the child if the child has lived with the relative for a period of at least one year immediately preceding the application'

NB. This changes the existing requirement for relatives that the child must have been living with them for a period of 3 years out of the last 5 and aligns relatives with local authority foster carers (for whom s.113 Adoption & Children Act 2002 reduced their qualifying period for s.8 Orders to 1 year)

Duration of Residence Order [s.37]

- S.9(6) Children Act 1989 Act (restriction on length of orders under s.8 of that Act) is amended so that a Residence Order (unlike other s.8 Orders) will last until the child is 18, unless the court directs that it should end earlier or another order is made that discharges it.

Special Guardianship Orders

Entitlement of Relative to Apply for a Special Guardianship Order [s.38]

■ S.14A(5) Children Act 1989 (persons entitled to apply for Special Guardianship Order) is amended, so that a relative with whom the child has lived for a period of at least 1 year immediately preceding the application is entitled to apply for a Special Guardianship Order.

PART 5

SUPPLEMENTARY, GENERAL & FINAL PROVISIONS

Orders, Regulations & Guidance [s.40]

- Any order or regulations made by the Secretary of State or the Welsh Ministers under this Act must be made by statutory instrument [s.40 (1)].

- A statutory instrument containing provision made by the Secretary of State under s.1(6) or (7) or s.12 may not be made unless a draft of the instrument has been laid before and approved by a resolution of each House of Parliament [s.40(2)].

- Any other statutory instrument containing provision made by the Secretary of State is subject to annulment in pursuance of a resolution of either House of Parliament [s.40(3)].

- A statutory instrument containing provision made by the Welsh Ministers under s.1(6) or (7) may not be made unless a draft of the instrument has been laid before and approved by a resolution of the National Assembly for Wales [s.40(4)].

- A statutory instrument containing provision made under s.13 may not be made unless:

  - A draft of the instrument has been laid before and approved by a resolution of the National Assembly for Wales, and
  - Having been so approved, has been laid before and approved by a resolution of each House of Parliament [s.40(5)]

- As soon as reasonably practicable after the resolution required by s.40(5)(a) has been passed, the First Minister must ensure that notice in writing of the resolution and a copy of the draft of the statutory instrument is sent to the Secretary of State [s.40(6)].

- On receipt of a draft of a statutory instrument under s.40(6) the Secretary of State must as soon as reasonably practicable lay it before each House of Parliament [s.40(7)].

- The latter paras. of s.40 (5), (6) and (7) cease to have effect on the making of an order under s.105 Government of Wales Act 2006 bringing the Assembly Act provisions into force [s.40(8)].

- In s.40(8) 'the Assembly Act provisions' has the same meaning as in the Government of Wales Act 2006 (see s.103(8) of that Act) [s.40(9)].

- Any other statutory instrument containing provision made by the Welsh Ministers is subject to annulment in pursuance of a resolution of the National Assembly for Wales [s.40(10)].

- S.40 (3) and (10) do not apply to a statutory instrument containing only provision made under s.44 [s.s.40(11)].

- Any power to make regulations under this Act includes power to make different provision for different cases and such supplemental or consequential provisions as appear to the Secretary of State or, as the case may, the Welsh Ministers to be appropriate [s.40(12)]

■ Any power under this Act to give guidance includes power to give different guidance for different cases [s.40 (13)].

Commencement [s.44]

- S.8 and Part 5 come into force on the day on which this Act is passed [s.44(1)].

- The reference in s.44(1) to this Part does not include:

  - Para. 4 of Schedule 2, which comes into force in accordance with s.44(9) and
  - S.42 and Sch. 3, which come into force in accordance with s.44 (3) and (4) [s.44(2)]

- In relation to Wales, the provisions specified in s.44(5) come into force on such day as the Welsh Ministers may by order appoint i.e.:

  - Parts 1 to 4 (except ss.8, 18, 19, 31 and 32);
  - S.42 and Sch. 3 [s.44(3);(5)]

- Otherwise the provisions of this Act come into force on such day as the Secretary of State may by order appoint [s.44(4)].

- An order under s.44 bringing s.11(2) into force in relation to Wales requires the consent of the Secretary of State [s.44(6)]

- An order under s.44 bringing ss.18 or 19 into force requires the consent of the Welsh Ministers [s.44(7)].

- Before making an order bringing ss.31 or 32 into force, the Secretary of State must consult the Welsh Ministers [s.44(8)].

■ Para.4 of Sch. 2 comes into force on the same day as s. 7(1) Carers and Disabled Children Act 2000 comes into force for the purpose of inserting s.17B into the Children Act 1989 Act in relation to Wales [s.44(9)].

■ An order under s.44 may appoint different days for different purposes or include transitional, saving or transitory provision [s.44(10)].

Appendix: CAE Publications

From CAE Ltd, Pantiles, Langham Road, Robertsbridge, East Sussex TN32 5EP, tel: 01580 880243 email: *childact@dial.pipex.com* or order via our secure on-line facility at *www.caeuk.org*

- Children Act 1989 in the Context of Human Rights Act 1998
- Children Act 2004
- Child Protection
- Residential Care of Children
- Fostering
- 'How Old Do I Have To Be?'
- Domestic Violence
- Sexual Offences Act 2003
- Childcare Act 2006
- Children & Young Persons Act 2008
- Safeguarding Vulnerable Groups Act 2006
- Assessment of Special Educational Needs
- ContactPoint

From CAE Scotland, 105 Bishops Park, Mid Calder, West Lothian, EH53 0SR, tel: 01506 883885 email: *childactScotland@dsl.pipex.com*

- The Children (Scotland) Act 1995 in The Context of the Human Rights Act 1998

Discounts on orders of 50 or more of any one title